ACCESSI

Accessioning

POEMS BY CHARLOTTE WETTON

THE EMMA PRESS

To Toby

☙

THE EMMA PRESS

First published in the UK in 2023 by The Emma Press Ltd.
Poems © Charlotte Wetton 2023.

ISBN 978-1-915628-13-8

A CIP catalogue record of this book
is available from the British Library.

Cover design by Reena Makwana.
Typeset by Normunds Ozols.

Printed and bound in the UK
by the Holodeck, Birmingham.

The Emma Press
theemmapress.com
hello@theemmapress.com
Birmingham, UK

CONTENTS

Scream

Thank God for the MOT expiring

                 and the tax-return deadline

and open windows we must rush to close against the rain

and customers

          especially awkward ones

who require attention to detail

                 and stop us thinking

about cliffs

       and how like skulls their faces are.

Go to places that demand perfunctory exchanges

drive-thrus, petrol stations

              where our lines are mapped

and it's all a bad acting gig, unpaid.

                   Don't imagine

lying down flat on the grass

the motorway verge or the kiddies' playground

so that truck drivers and waitresses and account executives

stop their vehicles

take their places
               widen the jaw

feel it bloom in the lungs and billow

a Zeppelin   a tsunami
                           an opera roiling out

a tent of red noise
               unravelled

flaming over the land.

The Artist Lives for a Time in Birmingham

The streets are littered with small bones;
rats come at night and carry them away.

He goes out to drive the flyovers. He loves their easy zoom,
the city falling past, the lights always Christmassy.

He rents a hangar in the Black Country for the artworks he hasn't made.
People chuck McBoxes out car windows.

In Alum Rock, a woman hangs out washing in gradations of colour,
mistaking her front yard for an important gallery.

White gulls bob on the reservoir clean as a picture-book
thinking of chip wrappers and congealed noodles.

The cellars flood, cold knifing through the floor. He invents
the word Meerkatism and carries it round for a while in a little basket.

He sits in his hangar enjoying the invisibility of installation.
He reckons he's making real progress. The seagulls keen like cats.

On the 53, he finds a hole in a woman's head and climbs in.
It's hot as a sauna. Does she really think that?!

Those without gardens can rent them on flat-bed trucks.
He publishes his posthumous memoirs; learns braille, just
in case.

He has a complete vision of his exhibition but doesn't write it down.
Then drinks himself sober. Do these gulls even know about the sea?

On the 53, a man groans and, when the Artist asks if he's OK,
says he's thinking about Monday: breaking up jukeboxes.

Weekly, the neighbours pile their bin bags in front of his house for collection.
He writes the catalogue: *metal walls (mixed media)*.

The garden is a box of face-high brambles.
Are these gulls a portent of his future by the sea?

Posting Index Cards Home

Kommetjie

A handstand in the sea   the flare of wavering legs
worrying is a type of fortune-telling
a fat woman climbing onto a lilo like a child
I'm writing a list   things to worry about later.
/
Worrying is a type of [non]fortune-telling
naked children about to fly   in orange water-wings
I'm writing a list   things to worry about later
an old couple swimming out to sea.
/
Naked children about to fly   in orange water-wings
worrying about something is not the same as doing something
an old couple swimming out to sea
worrying confers control   and prevents surprises.
/
Worrying about something is not the same as doing something
breasts slung in bikinis like little hammocks
worrying confers control   and prevents surprises
we're all braised shrimps in a pie dish   salt.
/

Breasts slung in bikinis like little hammocks
the horizon drawn with a thick blue crayon and a ruler
we're all braised shrimps in a pie dish   salt
I feel safe when I'm worrying   sea bird human cries.
/
The horizon drawn with a thick blue crayon and a ruler
a fat woman climbing onto a lilo like a child
I feel [un]safe when I'm worrying   sea bird human cries
a handstand in the sea   the flare of wavering legs.

Commissioning a Map

West Yorkshire

The cartographer and I have had a tiff:
I don't appreciate his profession,
my slapdash approach to boundaries is troubling,
the distance the crow flies is not the same as walking.
But that's just fine because I
am more interested in flying than walking.
He explains my map is not to scale,
that I've mixed Northings with Eastings,
that A and B roads aren't choices made or unmade.
A variable of five degrees can be the difference
between success or failure.
But my concerns are not to scale and furthermore
I want the bridleways unbridled,
the best bacon sandwiches mapped,
where to go sledging and
what time not to walk alone at night.
Maps, he explains, don't do temporal,
and I say, well, the hydrographer did the whales
spouting beautifully in the ornamental lake.
He points out the hydrographer got lost
trying to draw an armada at the swimming pool
and asks me not to hopscotch on his grid lines.
He thinks I'm a slag heap (dis).

But he has plotted the silence of the moors
(marsh, reeds or saltings)
and the gorgeous swoop of the motorway.
The cartographer is sick of drawing dragons
and if I have that many dragons
there'll be no cattle left in Calderdale.
BS! I say. I'm the one making this map;
you're just my technical advisor. You need
more than technical, he says, more than advice.
It's true that there's a bubble in my compass.

Wish-bone

Having laid the table of myself, fear jiggles
around my breast-bone; in desperation

I go out and plunge both hands into the compost bin.
Poor little wobble heart, you are, after all, only mediocre,

poking and nosing, filching and finger dipping,
and all the ugly things set in gold frames.

Yet... I will boil a rainforest into jujubes,
singe your eyelashes with Catherine wheels,

vomit fireworks into your lap, burst
your eardrums from the inside, truffle-hogging

in obscure funnel-web nests of chatrooms,
ice-climbing in the wrong equipment

There's an unpleasant rapacity about you
Yes, I so badly want to be a wolf running through the night

but you're just someone who doesn't like offices,
blowing your nose and examining the tissue.

The Archivist's House

They broke down the door to the archivist's house,
two policemen and a social worker, and found
his stacks. Lists ran over window ledges,
skirting boards, between the lines of other lists:
Wanted and Unwanted Gifts, Money Spent and Regretted
spooling and spinning with threaded thought.

He'd sweated ink, breath fogged with it
and the notes fattening, continually multiplying:
Useful Objects Found in the Street, New Foods Tasted
meticulously catalogued, references numbered

                                                      but

lists flicker away into

                           Women Not Spoken To
                           Unsuccessful Job Interviews

each option classified

                     the next option and the next

                                     on deeper

into sub-categories

                     secondary indexes

self spread thin between choices
a lacewing smeared in a folio

Film Releases Missed
Unfinished Conversations

pigeon holes spill
                into white, rustling pages

unravelled
         lists tangle together
thickets of possibles choke up the passageways

box files split like fruit skins
               spongy and bulging
                          stacked sheets

                          shunting
                          into wadded heaps
                          pressed into mulch

only rat-runs between essential rooms now

thumbs and heels grease-soften the paper
                          moulding the lists
                          to a muffled cocoon

the fusty smell of his paper skins
the slow stifling heat
the weight.

Specimen Drawers

Ilfracombe Museum

A drawer marked *Wedding Cakes*: brown patchwork, glistening.
My eyes adjust. Flat squares of wedding cake, packed tight.
Dark spots of currants, beige icing, twirls of lace, silk flowers.
Couples' names and dates on hand-written labels, 1888, 1956.

*

Imagine it packed, chokingly, in the throat, powdering like
brown earth, weevils coiling. A long table – eating and talking
and laughing in bone-yellow dresses, crunching vitrified
marzipan and liver-spot raisins before swaying tiers of cakes,
mice burrowing. And a ghost band plays and the first dance is
danced forever and ever, souls tethered to a dozen village halls
and hotels – the missing slice.

*

Cake should not be an epitaph. It is made to crumble on the tongue, dispersed to cousins and aunts in white napkins, snuck out of tins and off sideboards by the large hands of greedy husbands. Eggs and flour. You cannot carve monuments in cake. You cannot engrave details of contracts. It should not last.

*

A wedding crasher, trophy-hunting up and down the Devon coast – evidence for his mates. A vampire groom, remarrying through centuries, knowing the grief to come. A bridesmaid, light on her feet in butterfly colours: *Put a slice under your pillow and you'll dream of your future husband.* And all night faces flicker like train windows through trees.

*

I Spit Cherry Stones into the Sea

Nafplion

Metallic domed church
on a blue hill.

My gold sandals
on a rock by the sea

like an advert.
I post photos up, curate

myself to myself.
Graffiti on a cactus.

The horses of the Madonna
all yelling in stereo.

Private Tour

Haworth

My mother asked if she could,
for a moment, lie
on the small hard sofa
where Emily Brontë died.
They said no.

Sketchbook #3: Self-portrait of the curator as an artist

having reviewed an exhibition of souls trapped in blackbirds' eggs / how come you can't do away with those little cream squares next to your paintings / all down the street the black mouths of the post boxes critiquing / the sketch-book is a sucky-blanket / that character in Bleak House in his cluttered accumulation of a junk shop failing to teach himself to read he was the artist at the centre of the novel / think longingly of cloisters / can I submit a cult as my final project / in the galleries I enjoy the white walls / those creating experimental art should first decide what knowledge they are testing / why is no-one bringing me warm milky drinks / I could frame a spider scrabbling in the skull forelegs wavering up the smooth walls / is this good enough do I pass / one finds one has so many needs / here is a map of my foot /

What's Left?

Museum of Cycladic Art, Athens

Hypotheses, supposition

minerals
crushed
on the interiors of bone tubes

                    used for transportation of
                    rare pigments

greenish stains of malachite
red ochre, cinnabar or azurite

colour decoration deduced

                  from patterns of erosion

renders
eyes, eyebrows,
bracelets, diadems.

It is unclear if they are hunters or warriors.

*

Grave goods

aryballoi
bucranium
core of obsidian

rich and poor graves

stone spindle-shaped beads and spoons
ellipsoidal veined stones.

Children are buried unfurnished.

*

Lacunae, omissions
art

schematic figures
                    gritty, poorly fired and lightly burnished

mortals or mythological beings
                            of probable apotropaic
                            character
divine escorts to the dead

corrosions and encrustations suggest
                            figurines face-down
                            in the grave

& artistic conservatism
                    associated with religious
                    depictions.

There are intermediate or transitional forms.

*

Traces of repair
objects of unknown use

evidence of metallurgical activities

knives, chisels, tweezers

copper weapons
calyx-shaped kylix
spool-shaped pyxides
phiale
       with double running spirals

                                  infilled with kaolin.

*

A depression in the ground

fossilised fruit seeds

a little jointed figure
                either a God or a toy

behind glass, back-lit
soft yellow light
on black.

The Cave-Precipice of Andritsa

Greece

In the last quarter of the 6th Century AD
thirty-three Christians,
mostly women and children,

descended fourteen metres
to the cave-precipice of Andritsa.

The difficulty of access implies irregular use.

They had buckles and needles and lamps,
amphorae for water and oil,
numerous coins, a goat for milk.

Coin hoards are indicative
of political instability.

They had earrings and brooches and rings
and a bronze processional cross.

The absence of cooking equipment
means the refuge was temporary.

They'd hung bells round the necks of their children
to ward off evil spirits.

They had several small knives and one spear-head
found at the cave mouth,
which is suggestive of hostile threat.

The presence of keys shows they intended to go home.

The skeletal remains were clustered in small groups,
their pots leaning against the cave walls
as if to collect water droplets,

their cross still standing
between bronze Communion vessels.

None of the thirty-three skeletons
display marks of violence;

no funerary practices were discovered
upon inspection of the site.

It appears they lay down in family groups,
unable or unwilling to leave the cave,
clay lamps stuttering in the dark.

Slave Lodge

Cape Town

they have made a column of names
perspex   eight feet tall

Domingo of Bengal
Sijmen Ham van Madagascar
Magdalena Smith

the historians have come with their tweezers and soft brushes

Maria van de Kaap
Mira van Java

newly forged names with a hasp and a hinge
circular names that lead back to the lodge

Moses van Macassar
January of Malabaar

pick up a white man's story   squeeze it   harder
scour his account books   floor plans
                    his last will and testament

Maria van Ceijlon
Titus van Mallebaar

crack it open and the smallest Russian doll tumbles out
black female   bequeathed furniture
                  various household items

Diana van Krankebaar
Cornelia van Nan

the historians are clothing the stripped
                        their coat-hanger names

Manuel van Negombo
Susanna van Semesia
unnamed of Madagascar
Johannes van Batavia
no name of Angola

Rag

The dead women are laid to rest in filing cabinets,
they wash down windows with vinegar.
The dead women, folded inside a man's shoes,
give him that extra inch.
The dead women thicken the plot,
kill wasps and reflect badly on the department.
The dead women are lit spills.
They are a mobile of planets hanging
from the ceiling of class 3b,
as part of their space project.
The dead women become overnight celebrities,
get recycled, line rabbit hutches and run for weeks.
They keep the glass flush on a framed print
of Krishna and the gopis.
They are carpet-backing and beginner's origami.
They are a clever red herring,
dress maker's cut-outs,
a money-spinner and wrap fish.
The dead women lie on the dashboard
of a white van in the sun
and the dead women had it coming.
Tied with string, they cover fruitcake in a cool oven.
The dead women hold broken glass,
then twirl downstream as tiny boats.

They flatten themselves on the chimney breast
and the fire draws.
The dead women need cataloguing.
The dead women slide off the seats and litter the train.
The dead women blow in the wind.

Exhibit A.2412.331:
Sloth skeleton

Manchester Museum

Two curators
palm-cup his skull
cradle the descant of his spine

gently they lift and loop
his elegant hooked toes
to a perspex cross

swung supine
small as a child

he is fretwork
unfleshed
an armful of air

snappable.

Stripped to articulated mechanics
jointings and engines
load-bearing carabiner claws

exacting requirements
gleam warm-white.

The curators are skilled, trained
and the need for conservation
axiomatic

easily they cherish his clean bones

and in the quiet museum
tongue his soft name

sibilant hiss of Eden
thick plummet of felled forest

his muzzle turned to the wall.

When This is Over We'll Memorialise

young handlers with fragile bodies
who felt a bond with every orca,
dazzling in black and white wetsuits
and brilliant smiles, soaring upwards
astride the sleek kinetic muscle
of tamed apex predators: Skana, Hyak II,
Kandu V who hang stationary in sea pens
chewing on concrete walls and metal gates
who come to the whistle like dogs.
We'll commemorate Hugo, Nepo,
Kandu VII whose vocalisations
scientists are reluctant to call language
but concede are cultural. Who feed
on eagle rays, hammerheads, leopard seals
and travel a hundred miles a day.
Keanu, Winston, Nootka IV who share
with us the neural spindle cells
needed for love and attachment,
whose families are decimated.
When this is over there'll be plaques
commemorating the separation of Kasatka
from her calf and the calm courage
of Ken Peters, treading water, reventilating
before Kasatka drags him to the tank floor again.

We'll remember Tamarie Tollison
screaming while Orkid and Splash circled;
Joanne Hey, pinned against the tank wall 'till
someone thrust their fist in Kandu's blowhole;
remember Jonathan Smith, waving to the crowd
before Keanu pulled him down a second time.
There'll be monuments to the colleagues
who yanked each other from the water
by fractured arms, spotters who ran for life-rings,
who tried distractions, hand-slaps
then a metal pole to prise open Shamu's mouth.
Another monument for the families
sitting in tribunals, being told 'handler error'
and one for the broken matrilines,
the breach, the spy-hop, the tail-slap.
A memorial for Tilikum's mother
sewn full of rocks, tail chained to an anchor,
and for Tilikum's pod, who stayed for hours calling
while the females were slaughtered.
And a memorial for those killed by Tilikum
Dawn Brancheau, Keltie Byrne, Alexis Martinez,
for the moment, near consciousness,
the dark bulk of the orca above, when drawing breath
is suddenly involuntary, the throat relaxes,
the ocean pours into the lungs.

ACKNOWLEDGEMENTS

My thanks to the editors who have previously published these poems:

'Commissioning a Map' featured in *Many: The 2020 Manchester Anthology*.

'The Cave-Precipice of Andritsa' appeared in a special-edition anthology pamphlet for The British Library, celebrating the Michael Marks Pamphlet Awards.

'The Archivist's House' formed part of my first pamphlet *I Refuse to Turn into a Hatstand*, published by Calder Valley Poetry.

A different version of 'Rag' has been published in *Poetry Wales*.

'Slave Lodge' featured in *The Kindling*.

ABOUT THE POET

Charlotte Wetton's first pamphlet *I Refuse to Turn into a Hat-Stand* (Calder Valley Poetry) won the Michael Marks Award for Best Poetry Pamphlet in 2017.

She is a PhD candidate at the University of Manchester and lives in West Yorkshire.

She can be found on Twitter @CharPoetry